Keys to the Kingdom

Bob Tate

TEACH Services, Inc.
P U B L I S H I N G
www.TEACHServices.com • (800) 367-1844

Copyright © 2019 Bob Tate
Copyright © 2019 TEACH Services, Inc.
ISBN-13: 978-1-4796-1045-7 (Paperback)
ISBN-13: 978-1-4796-1046-4 (ePub)

TEACH Services, Inc.
P U B L I S H I N G
www.TEACHServices.com • (800) 367-1844

"And this gospel of the kingdom will be preached in all the world as a witness to all the nations, and then the end will come."

(Matthew 24:14)

PROLOGUE

GOING NUCLEAR

With all the problems in the world today—including the talk of nuclear war between man to destroy man—I'm thankful for the evidence of a spiritual force even greater than that. More specifically, I'm thankful for that which is inherent in the name of Jesus Christ, who is the POWER of God and the WISDOM of God (1 Corinthians 1:18, 24). This is not that of the world, but God's unique way of saving people.

When we proclaim HIM, we are proclaiming the AUTHORITY in His name. He alone is the One who begets new life in people. He alone is the POWER of God to salvation for everyone who believes (Romans 1:16).

This little booklet contains a series of studies focusing on the preaching of Jesus.

The Christian religion is more than just a system of beliefs. It centers in the person of the MAN who is GOD, the SAVIOR, and everlasting FATHER.

With that in mind, starting with those nearest and dearest to you, let's all do what we can to share the POWER.

The Christian religion is more than just a system of beliefs.
It centers in the person of the MAN who is GOD, the SAVIOR, and everlasting FATHER.

THE GOSPEL

Jesus was born into this world miraculously by the Holy Spirit. He had no human father.

He lived a perfect, sinless life. His ministry was one of power, with great signs, miracles, and wonders that God performed through Him, affirming Him before the people. However, the leaders of that day plotted against Him and had Him murdered by crucifixion. But God raised Him up again.

After revealing Himself to more than five hundred people over a period of forty days (1 Cor. 15:6), He was miraculously caught up in a cloud to the throne of God in heaven, where He is alive today (Acts 1:9–11). All power and authority in heaven and on earth have been given to Him.

And being in such a high and exalted state, He is now commanding men everywhere to REPENT of their sins and turn to God with works of evidence, because He has appointed a day in which He will judge the world in righteousness (Acts 17:30, 31; see also Acts 26:20).

"REPENT, and let every one of you be BAPTIZED in the name of Jesus Christ for the remission of sins" and the promise is: "You shall receive the GIFT of the Holy Spirit."

Again he says, "Repent therefore and be converted, that your sins may be blotted out, so that TIMES OF REFRESHING may come from the presence of the Lord" (Acts 2:37, 38; Acts 3:19).

"The word is near you, in your mouth and in your heart (that is, the word of faith which we preach): that if you confess with your mouth the Lord Jesus and believe in your heart that God has raised Him from the dead, you will be saved. For with the heart one BELIEVES unto righteousness, and with the mouth CONFESSION is made unto salvation" (Romans 10:8–10).

"For 'whoever CALLS on the name of the Lord shall be saved'" (Romans 10:13).

"See, I have set before you an open door..."

(Revelation 3:8)

"I am the door. If anyone enters by Me, he will be saved…"

(John 10:9)

Preaching Jesus

"For though you might have ten thousand instructors in Christ, yet you do not have many fathers; For in CHRIST JESUS I have begotten you through the GOSPEL."

(1 Corinthians 4:15)

Jesus Preached Himself

"And beginning at Moses and all the Prophets, He expounded to them in all the Scriptures the things concerning HIMSELF."

(Luke 24:27; see also Luke 24:44–47)

HIS DISCIPLES PREACHED JESUS

"And daily in the temple, and in every house, they did not cease teaching and preaching JESUS as the CHRIST" (Acts 5:42).

"Then Philip went down to the city of Samaria and preached CHRIST to them" (Acts 8:5).

"Then Philip opened his mouth and … preached JESUS to him" (Acts 8:35).

"Christ had to suffer … and saying, 'this JESUS whom I preach to you is the CHRIST'" (Acts 17: 3).

"From Jerusalem and round about…I have fully preached the gospel of CHRIST…" (Romans 15:19).

"We preach CHRIST crucified…" (1 Corinthians 1:23).

"I determined not to know anything among you except JESUS CHRIST and HIM crucified" (1 Corinthians 2:2).

"For I delivered to you FIRST OF ALL … that CHRIST died for our sins … and that He was buried, and that He rose again the third day … so we preach and so you believed" (1 Corinthians 15:3, 4, 11).

"For we do not preach ourselves, but CHRIST JESUS the LORD…" (2 Corinthians 4:5).

"It pleased God, who…called me through His grace, to reveal His Son in me, that I might preach HIM among the Gentiles…" (Galatians 1:15, 16).

"Whether in pretense or in truth, CHRIST is preached; and in this I rejoice…" (Philippians 1: 18).

"…CHRIST in you, the hope of glory. HIM we preach…" (Colossians 1:27, 28).

"Then I saw another angel flying in the midst of heaven, having the EVERLASTING GOSPEL to preach to those who dwell on the earth…" (Revelation 14:6).

"In Him we have redemption through His blood, the forgiveness of sins, according to the riches of His grace..."

(Ephesians 1:7)

"In Him you also trusted, after you heard the word of truth, the gospel of your salvation..."

(Ephesians 1:13)

"Now to Him who is able to establish you according to my gospel and the preaching of Jesus Christ … and by the Prophetic Scriptures made known to all nations…"

(Romans 16:25, 26)

"These are the words which I spoke to you… that all things must be fulfilled which were written in the Law of Moses and the Prophets and the Psalms concerning Me."

(Luke 24:44)

PREACHING JESUS FROM THE OLD TESTAMENT

He would be born of a virgin mother. (Isaiah 7:14; Luke 1:26–35)

His coming would be heralded by a star. (Numbers 24:17; Matthew 2:1, 2)

He would be the king of Israel. (Numbers 24:17; Matthew 27:37)

He would be born in Bethlehem. (Micah 5:2; Luke 2:1–7)

His mission would be to liberate. (Isaiah 61:1; Luke 4:16–21)

He would be rejected by His nation. (Isaiah 53:3; Luke 23:18–23)

He would be betrayed by a friend. (Psalm 41:9; Luke 22:47, 48)

He would be forsaken by God. (Psalm 22:1; Matthew 27:45, 46)

He would be bruised but crush His opponent. (Genesis 3:15; Hebrews 2:14, 15)

He would be wounded for our sins. (Isaiah 53:5; 1 Peter 2:24)

His life would be terminated for us. (Isaiah 53:8; Romans 5:6–8)

His death would be by crucifixion. (Psalm 22:16; Luke 23:33)

They would cast lots for His clothing. (Psalm 22:18; Matthew 27:35)

He would be counted among the wicked. (Isaiah 53:9; Matthew 27:38)

He would be buried in a rich man's grave. (Isaiah 53:9; Matthew 27:57–60)

He would be resurrected. (Psalm 16:9, 10; Acts 2:22–24)

He would ascend to Heaven. (Psalm 24:7–10; Acts 1:9–11)

He would sit at God's right hand. (Psalm 110:1; Mark 16:19)

THE DIVINITY OF CHRIST

His name is called Emmanuel [God with us]. (Isaiah 7:14)

He has existed from eternity. (Micah 5:2)

He is called the Mighty God, Everlasting Father. (Isaiah 9:6)

He was in the form of God. (Philippians 2:6)

All the fullness of God dwelt in Him. (Colossians 1:19; Colossians 2: 9, 10)

He is the Word of God. (John 1:1)

He made the worlds. (Hebrews 1:2)

He sustains the universe. (Hebrews 1:3)

He appeared as a man. (Philippians 2:8; John 1:14)

All the angels of God worship Him. (Hebrews 1:6)

God calls Him God. (Hebrews 1:8)

He will rule forever. (Hebrews 1:8)

SALVATION THROUGH FAITH IN CHRIST ALONE

Sin is breaking the law [lawlessness]. (1 John 3:4)

All have sinned. (Romans 3:23)

The result of sin is death. (Romans 6:23)

Death happens when blood is shed. (Hebrews 9:22)

The life is in the blood. (Leviticus 17:11)

Daily offerings of shed blood provided ongoing cleansing from sin. (Exodus 29:38, 39)

Sin offerings of shed blood were made individually. (Leviticus 4:27–33)

Jesus is the sacrificial lamb that shed His blood for the sins of the world. (John 1:29)

He was wounded and cut off for our sins. (Isaiah 53:4–8)

He Himself bore our sins in His own body. (1 Peter 2:24)

Through His blood we have the forgiveness of sins. (Colossians 1:14)

He rose from the dead. (Matthew 28:6)

He died for our sins and rose again. (1 Corinthians 15:1–4)

He died, rose, and lived again. (Romans 14:9)

He destroyed the devil and released his prisoners. (Hebrews 2:14, 15)

He has abolished death and gifted eternal life to every believer. (2 Timothy 1:10)

His resurrection is the assurance of our own. (1 Thessalonians 4:14; 1 Thessalonians 5:9, 10; 2 Corinthians 4:14)

Whoever comes to Him will be received. (John 6:37)

Whoever believes in Him will never perish. (John 3:16)

Everyone who believes in Him has passed from death to life. (John 5:24)

We have peace with God when we believe in Jesus. (Romans 5:1)

BAPTISM: THE SIGN OF FAITH AND REPENTANCE

Jesus was baptized as our example. (Matthew 3:13–15)

By one Spirit we are all baptized into one body. (1 Corinthians 12:13)

We are baptized into His death. (Romans 6:3)

We are buried with Him through baptism. (Romans 6:4)

We are raised from the dead to walk in newness of life. (Romans 6:4)

All who believe and are baptized will be saved. (Mark 16:16)

All should repent and be baptized. (Acts 2:36–38)

We should believe with ALL OUR HEART. (Acts 8:37)

We should verbally CONFESS the Lord Jesus. (Acts 8:37; Philippians 2:11)

The Holy Spirit convicts that Jesus is the Lord. (1 Corinthians 12:3)

Whoever BELIEVES in Him shows he is born of God. (1 John 5:1)

THE RETURN OF CHRIST

He promised to return. (John 14:1–3)

The righteous living will be waiting for Him. (Isaiah 25:9)

The righteous dead will be resurrected. (1 Thessalonians 4:16)

The dead will awake and sing. (Isaiah 26:19)

Many shall awake to everlasting life. (Daniel 12:1, 2)

The living righteous will be translated. (1 Corinthians 15:50–55)

The risen dead and living righteous will be caught up to meet Him. (1 Thessalonians 4:17)

He will come from the east. (Matthew 24:27)

The stars, moon, and sun will shake. (Matthew 24:29)

There will be a great earthquake. (Revelation 6:12)

The sky will recede. (Revelation 6:14)

He will appear in heaven. (Matthew 24:30)

The world will mourn. (Matthew 24:30)

We will see Him coming on the clouds. (Matthew 24:30)

He will come with power and great glory. (Matthew 24:30)

Every eye will see Him. (Revelation 1:7)

He will come in flaming fire. (2 Thessalonians 1:7, 8)

His coming will be a storm of burning turbulence. (Psalm 50:3)

He comes to take vengeance on unbelievers. (2 Thessalonians 1:8)

He will punish them with eternal destruction. (2 Thessalonians 1:9)

The wicked will hide from His face. (Revelation 6:15)

They will pray for the mountains to fall on them. (Revelation 6:16)

The earth will be broken and split open. (Isaiah 24:19–22)

The Lord will empty the earth. (Isaiah 24:1–3)

EPILOGUE

HANDING OFF THE BATON

In early America, during the days of slavery, history tells us that some were deliberately denied an education. It was said that when an enslaved person learned or was taught to read, it became his or her responsibility to teach someone else. This principle is what gave rise to the phrase, "Each one, teach one."

In the same way today, whenever anyone is taught about Jesus and believes in Him, it becomes his or her responsibility to teach someone else.

This is emphasized in 2 Timothy 2:2, easily remembered as the 2,2,2 way: "And the things that you have heard from me among many witnesses, COMMIT THESE to faithful men who will be able to teach others also."

The lessons in this booklet are designed to assist you in COMMITTING these things to others. Jesus is the heart and POWER of salvation. As you share Him with others you are giving them the keys to the door of the kingdom of God.

May you be blessed as you reach out and touch others and teach those others to be teachers.

"And the Spirit and the bride say, "Come!" And let him who hears say, "Come!" And let him who thirsts come. Whoever desires, let him take the water of life freely."

(Revelation 22:17)

Would you like more information on what the Bible says regarding the following topics?

- How do I live as a Christian?
- What happens when we die?
- Tell me about end time events.
- What is the mark of the beast?
- How do I find security in this world?
- Which day is the Sabbath?

**For the answers to these questions
and many others, as well as for information
on receiving Bible studies, please visit
https://www.bibleinfo.com**

TEACH Services, Inc.
P U B L I S H I N G

We invite you to view the complete
selection of titles we publish at:
www.TEACHServices.com

We encourage you to write us
with your thoughts about this,
or any other book we publish at:
info@TEACHServices.com

TEACH Services' titles may be purchased in
bulk quantities for educational, fund-raising,
business, or promotional use.
bulksales@TEACHServices.com

Finally, if you are interested in seeing
your own book in print, please contact us at:
publishing@TEACHServices.com
We are happy to review your manuscript at no charge.

www.ingramcontent.com/pod-product-compliance
Lightning Source LLC
Chambersburg PA
CBHW040833110426

42739CB00036B/3479